the
book
of light

Illuminate Your Life with Self-Love

nia the light

HAY HOUSE

Carlsbad, California • New York City
London • Sydney • New Delhi

this book belongs to
a Queen named

....

Published in the United Kingdom by:
Hay House UK Ltd, The Sixth Floor, Watson House,
54 Baker Street, London W1U 7BU
Tel: +44 (0)20 3927 7290; Fax: +44 (0)20 3927 7291; www.hayhouse.co.uk

Published in the United States of America by:
Hay House Inc., PO Box 5100, Carlsbad, CA 92018-5100
Tel: (1) 760 431 7695 or (800) 654 5126
Fax: (1) 760 431 6948 or (800) 650 5115; www.hayhouse.com

Published in Australia by:
Hay House Australia Pty. Ltd, 18/36 Ralph St, Alexandria NSW 2015
Tel: (61) 2 9669 4299; Fax: (61) 2 9669 4144; www.hayhouse.com.au

Published in India by:
Hay House Publishers India, Muskaan Complex,
Plot No.3, B-2, Vasant Kunj, New Delhi 110 070
Tel: (91) 11 4176 1620; Fax: (91) 11 4176 1630; www.hayhouse.co.in

A catalogue record for this book is available from the British Library.

Tradepaper ISBN: 978-1-78817-392-6
E-book ISBN: 978-1-78817-396-4
Audiobook ISBN: 978-1-78817-502-9

Printed and bound in Italy by Graphicom

contents

This book tells the story of the lessons
I've learnt on my journey of self-love.

Some you may have learnt,
some you may be learning, and
some you're yet to learn.

I hope you enjoy this book
as I enjoyed creating it.
It's yours to doodle over,
to cry with, to travel with,
and to absorb light with.

love and light,

Niathelight

hello, beautiful

Before I get to hear your incredible story and learn more about you, I thought I'd share parts of my journey that have all aligned so perfectly, inspiring each and every page of this book.

I think it's important that I take you back to one of the most significant days of my life. The day I let go.

The room was warm and filled with all the people I love. They sat patiently waiting for me to cut my hair. The sound of the snipping scissors got louder, and everyone held their breath, watching. It was as though the golden locks of hair falling toward the floor were revealing a part of my soul for everyone beside me to see. Cutting that first piece of hair was like removing some kind of pain I'd been holding on to all of my life, the second felt like releasing the heartbreak I never quite got over, and the third reminded me that all I am and all I want to be wasn't within my hair. It was within me.

I thought I'd prepared myself for this moment, but I really wasn't ready for the true feeling of letting go. I hadn't felt this vulnerable since I fell over in the playground as a small child and bruised my knees. My mother comforted me then, just as she did now. When I turned toward the mirror, everyone waited to see my reaction, waited for me to see myself; this was the moment when I saw Nia. I loved what I saw. I thought that snipping off my hair and letting go of something I'd depended on for so long would somehow instantly release pain or hurt. Yet it didn't. In fact it started to unravel different aspects of me that I hadn't met or learnt to love, and I found that self-love is truly a journey and not a destination. The beautiful thing about this journey is that as you read this, you'll realize that I'm still on it. I'm still discovering who I was, who I am, and who I want to be.

I used to devote hours to taking pictures of myself and my big blond curly hair, because for each "like" I received I'd feel an abundance of validation. This grew to become a very toxic relationship, as my perception of my beauty was now in the hands of other people.

The moment of realization occurred toward the middle of 2017. I'd embarked on two successful tours around the USA, Europe, and Africa where I'd been hosting events for women of color to embrace who they are. On my return home, I came to understand how much of the world I'd captured with my phone camera but not experienced. I was no longer living my life for me but for everyone else.

I wore my hair loose in its glorious mane every day, and it slowly became my uniform and my blanket of comfort. When I cut it off and removed my uniform, I lost that source of validation and with it my whole sense of self. To rediscover who I was, I made the big decision to remove from my life everything that I depended on to validate my beauty. And so, on January 21, 2018, I cut off my hair—the hair I thought had given me billboards across the USA, enough money to travel the world, features in magazines, and the ability to live a spontaneous life. I know I'll never forget this fearless moment as it also marked the start of my journey of self-love.

Since that day, I've been learning to love my real self. The self with stretch marks that symbolize my journey from girl to woman, and my acne that tells me when it's time to slow down and nourish my body with healthy food, and the hair that grows no matter how many times I try to remove it with wax.

The idea of this book has been within me for many years. Every evening I write in my journal, discussing my day and talking to my younger self. This has become my therapy. We don't realize how much we grow through each day or how many amazing things we achieve. We're so focused on tomorrow that we forget about today. This is why I love writing, living through my inner child by taking Polaroid pictures and sticking them in my journal, and keeping plane tickets to remember the trips I took. It reminds me of my growth and how amazing life can truly be.

The Book of Light is your very own "like" button, your internal power-up, and your safe space in which to begin exploring who you are. As you work through this book, I want you to share your true self by documenting your experiences of self-love, living your best flaw-filled life, and knowing that as a woman you're always growing and learning. You should be proud of that.

The beautiful illustrations throughout the book will accompany our journey together. This will be a safe and peaceful space to help us connect with something far deeper than pixels.

The Book of Light will give you inspiration to love who you are.

The Book of Light will remind you to be your friend.

The Book of Light will help you to reflect on your journey of the past and your ambitions for the future.

Queens, are you ready to discover your light?

chapter 1
self

I'm so excited to begin this journey with you. As I share my evolving journey, I want you to share yours, too. I've put together some of the most significant lessons I've learnt on my journey of womanhood and, although I still have a lot to learn, I'm grateful for the woman I am today. This chapter is all about getting to know you and the wonderful beam of light that you are.

One of the first things I did on my journey was identify who I am, and with that discovery I was able to evolve and love the aspects of myself that I hadn't in a very long time. I was also able to navigate through life with confidence. Pain taught me how to heal, and joy taught me how to embrace each part of who I am. Life is always teaching me things about myself, and I've learnt along the way to never take those lessons for granted.

This journey to self-worth, self-love, and self-power is the most important one you'll ever embark on. Once you know who you are, no-one can take that away from you. It's your true power. It's the strength you'll draw on to create boundaries for yourself. It's the determination you'll have to pursue the dreams you spend hours visualizing. It's the sensitivity you'll have to love and care for others.

Let's begin this beautiful journey. I'm so happy to be joining you.

the power of you

Life is a never-ending journey of discovering who you are and who you aspire to be. The fun part about life is that we have the ability to change and evolve whenever you want. The girl you were five years ago isn't the woman you are today. That's to be celebrated and acknowledged anytime you feel down about the expectations you created for yourself.

When I think of who I am, my natural instinct has always been to think of my physical attributes, my career, and all the things I've achieved, or even the people I surround myself with. I was attached to the idea of being busy all the time and doing things because of the validation that came with that. But those things aren't me, nor do they define me. Everything I am is within me. I choose who I am because I know myself the best and I've known myself the longest.

What do you think of when you think of who you are? What's the first thing that comes to mind? I always find it interesting to see how people define themselves and where these thoughts come from. We're so fixated on wanting to be defined by our achievements and our triumphs. It gives us a sense of belonging—knowing we're embraced by a community in which people may have the same interests as us or feel the same way about certain things as we do. But no one is like you, and constantly striving to be accepted by others is an unhealthy cycle that will never empower you.

I've had such an insightful 23 years with myself. Being questioned about my cultural mix has taught me to embrace it. I've learnt how to turn my weaknesses and insecurities into strengths, and I've learnt to see my light, even in a dimly lit room. It's been important for me to change my narrative and how I react to the things that will eventually empower me. Nothing happens *to* you, it happens *for* you.

The journey begins once you learn to accept and forgive yourself for who you are. It begins once you learn to speak to yourself with kindness. We all have things about our bodies that we wish were bigger, smaller, smoother, or clearer, but those are the things that make us who we are. If I've learnt anything, it's that even when we attain the things we wish for we'll want more. So be sure to pause and embrace every single part of your journey.

I'm currently in a space of embracing my body for what it does rather than what it looks like. Every day I'm able to see the world with freedom, I'm able to taste foods that make me feel good, I'm able to touch people with my words, and feel textures or see sunsets that make me stand still. My mind and body hold so many stories that I can rewind and watch in times of reflection, in times of stillness, and in times of peace.

choose your own qualities

We learn so much from our parents and we mirror so much of who they are. As we get older, it's our choice to unlearn their habits or embrace the parts of them that give us joy. I love that I have qualities of both my mum and dad, as I know I'll always have parts of them with me as I journey through life. I have my mum's strength and ability to walk into a room and find a friend, and I have my dad's sensitivity and drive to create something.

I admire my mother's style and I always try to emulate her timeless sense of fashion. I know that when I have daughters, I'll teach them how to present themselves as Queens just as she taught me. But I'll unlearn how open and giving she was, as I saw how much it hurt her when people didn't reciprocate that same love and energy.

I admire my father's humor and how he sees the best in every situation. I love how much he values quality time and shows appreciation for the little things. So I'll teach my sons how to live life with adventure and freedom, but I'll unlearn the way he wasn't able to express his feelings and instead kept them to himself to avoid confrontation.

When you think of your parents or your loved ones, what qualities do you admire about them? What do you want to unlearn? Reflect on who they are and how they've influenced you.

who are you?

As a child, I used to love making mind maps. Writing is a way in which I can articulate my thoughts without the fear of judgment. Whenever I need to reset myself mentally, I create a mind map to help me get clear on how I'm feeling or what I want to achieve, especially if I need a source of inspiration.

Consider the journey you've been on so far in your life, and take some time to reflect on who you are, what you want to do, and what you love most about yourself. We often downplay our attributes, or wait for someone else to highlight them because we don't want to appear vain, but if we don't know who we are, how can we expect anyone else to? Think of the people who have taught you significant lessons in life and take a moment to appreciate them.

Knowing where I've come from has had a huge impact on how I navigate through life. I know the journey my grandmother from Zimbabwe went on so that she could do more for her family. She often reminds me to strive for more. I know how much my grandfather loved to laugh and enjoy the simple things in life, so when things become stressful I always sit still and embrace where I am in that moment.

When I feel stressed, I often mentally take myself back to a park I visited as a child. It reminds me of a time when I used to dream big and had no fear.

If you don't have that safe space, it's time to create one for yourself.

What difference do you want to make in the world?

....

....

Which country
or countries do you
come from?

....

....

Who has made a big
impact in your life?

....

....

....

....

....

....

....

Where is your
happy place?

....

....

....

What do you admire about yourself?

....

....

....

know where you've come from

A few years ago, I was on a retreat and in a very fragile mental space. I was having my busiest year to date, and it had sparked a depression that contributed so much to the woman I am today. During the retreat we were asked to reflect on where we'd come from and our journey to get where we were. Life is always moving so fast and we're so focused on the future that we forget what happened in the past, especially if it caused us trauma or reminds us of pain.

I decided to write down in detail all the moments that led to my significant memories. Sometimes we forget to acknowledge our triumphs and how many battles we've won, so I wrote about the good ones as well as the bad. This really helped me to understand why I'm the way I am.

From my memories I created a time line which you can see on the next page. This helped me to understand how strong I am, and how some situations may have contributed to the way I feel about myself.

It's time for you to change the narrative and give yourself the freedom to be who you are. Create your own time line by looking back at your journey and acknowledging where you've come from. You can't know who you are without knowing where you've been. This process might trigger you, and if it does, just take a moment to breathe and let it out, and then come back to the exercise when you're ready.

my time line

6 June 1997
I was born!

My friends at school made it apparent that I was different and didn't look like them. I began to question why I was mixed race and didn't have hair like everyone else.

4

6

11

I traveled to Zimbabwe and connected with my mother's culture. I remember playing in the garden with all the neighborhood kids.

I went to secondary (middle) school, making new friends and growing up.

I had my first job in a shoe shop which taught me a lot about hard work and earning money.

I traveled to the USA for Happy FroDay and worked at events for women with natural hair.

17

I went to sixth form college and gained a lot of confidence with my natural hair journey.

I got my driving license and bought a very old and broken car.

I cut off all my relaxed hair and started my natural hair journey.

My acne became severe. I went through depression, missed days off school, and didn't want to be around anyone.

12

15

16

I began my skincare journey and tried to heal my acne.

I had my first boyfriend, designed my own prom dress, graduated school, discovered Instagram, and started watching YouTube videos about curly hair.

I built my social media brand and started working with cool companies.

I had a billboard feature on Times Square and had my heart broken.

I graduated university.

18

20

21

I cut off my hair and began my journey of self-love.

I moved into my first apartment.

I am who I
choose to be.

No one thing
can define me.

be true to yourself

Sometimes, when we make decisions in life, we seek some kind of approval from the people we look up to. When I was 16, I began thinking about my future and the direction I wanted to take. I had so many voices feeding me with different things. Some thought it would be best to go to university, and others said it was a waste of time. The most wise thing anyone said was that whatever decision I made would lead me to wherever I needed to go.

My mother was adamant that I went to university to experience the opportunities she never had, whereas my father wanted me to pursue my passion and thought that university was a waste of time. I chose university because I wanted to make my mother happy. I strived for her approval for a long time in my life because I looked up to her and admired what she'd achieved.

I don't believe in looking back and having regrets about the decisions I've made because nothing you do can take you back to change them. But you can change how you feel and what you do in this very moment. In the end I left university with a degree, and the knowledge that I could do anything as I'd overcome so many obstacles during those years. University taught me how to keep balanced, and now, whenever I have an abundance of projects to complete or tasks to fulfill, I know I can achieve them because university taught me how.

My sense of achievement on graduation day is something I'll never take for granted because I knew how proud my mum and dad were. But I also felt proud of myself—I knew that I'd chosen my own career to embark on, and also that I could still devote time to what truly gave me joy.

Different people enhance different parts of ourselves. I have a variety of friends who all share so many unique features and my energy is heightened whenever I'm around them. It's important to pay attention to how you feel about yourself when you're around different people. If you feel down or unappreciated, ask yourself why you continue to surround yourself with that energy when it could be replaced with the uplifting energy of people who embrace you for you.

I know I'm around the wrong people when I forget how to be myself and I mold my features to please them. This is draining, but it's taught me that some people love you for who you are, and others have an image of you that they want you to fulfill.

Be yourself, whatever that feels like and whatever it looks like in your head. Change your style as many times as you like and sign up for any hobbies that inspire you. Always choose yourself first because, in the end, you'll only be left with those memories. So make them good ones.

choose yourself first

What's your
true passion?

....
....
....
....

When was the last time
you did something
for approval from
someone else?

....
....
....
....

If money wasn't
a thing, what
would you do?

....
....
....

When you think of your
dreams or who you want to
be, what comes to mind?

....
....
....
....

If you could spend a day with your
role model, who would it be and
what would you ask them?

....
....
....

If you could go
anywhere right now,
where would it be?

....
....
....

let your passion guide you

When we're influenced by others for a long period in our lives, it can be hard to think freely about who we really are and who we want to be. You're not the version of you that your mother has in her head, nor should you feel that you need to meet the expectations of your father.

As much as you might have a plan to finish school and find a job in a particular field, along the way you might find something else that sparks joy for you. You might have a plan, but life might have another plan for you. My younger self wanted to become a fashion designer, a singer, or even a dancer, but over time I found other passions. No one knew the Internet would evolve to help create businesses, nor did I know when I created my platform that it would give me the ability to travel the world.

Go with the flow of life and let it inspire you. The future isn't here yet, so live for the moment. Think about what you really enjoyed as a child and why it sparked joy for you. Take a moment to reflect on what excites you the most.

As an only child I was always drawing and writing because I spent a lot of time alone. Although I didn't grow to become an artist, I did grow to write this book and work with an illustrator to bring my ideas to life. My choice of projects has never been driven by money or material gain but by love and knowing that I can do what I want to do. So let your passion guide you, and do everything out of love.

choose you

I'm proud of myself. I'm proud of the woman I've become. Even when I didn't meet the expectations others had of me, I know I exceeded the ones I had of myself. It's so important to always choose you. When I wanted to cut my hair, I spoke to a few people about it and they were shocked, but afterward they saw my freedom and realized why I'd done it.

I knew how I felt about myself at that time and what I needed to do to grow and heal. From the outside I was living an amazing life, but I wasn't happy. Nothing materialistic impressed me, and that's when I realized I had to let go. My happiness had turned into quality time with my loved ones and feeling safe.

Others can advise you, but they'll never know how you truly feel. My parents feared that cutting my hair would bring my career to a standstill or that I'd lose what made my online presence so unique. I knew I was far more than my hair and I wanted to show myself that. I wanted to see myself and remember who I was. I'm grateful for that experience because now I feel so confident in who I am.

Now, I choose wisely who I listen to. Do they emulate the lifestyle I want to live? Do they embody the woman I want to become? I can't listen to someone who doesn't reflect the characteristics I want to embody.

Choose you. In every job you apply for and any adventure you embark on; always choose you. It's easy for others to project their fears and insecurities onto you as a way of protecting you, but there's a fine line between protection and possession.

Right now, you have the choice and the power to do what makes you feel good. Don't take that time for granted. It comes and goes so quickly, and you don't want to regret wasting this time wondering "what if." When I wanted to open my hair salon, I spoke to my dad and he told me that if I didn't do it now then I'd always live with the idea of what might have been. I knew it was the biggest investment I was going to make, but I felt so empowered seeing it come together.

When I look back at my life, I want to remember all the risks I took and how they became great accomplishments. I want to admire my strength to walk away from money and deals to choose inner peace. I want to acknowledge how brave I was to hop on flights by myself with such an eagerness to see and experience the world. I don't want to wish for that time back.

We only have one life in this body, so don't take for granted the time you have to make a difference here. Embrace your strengths and work on your weaknesses, for they shall guide you and help you become the Queen you already are.

chapter 2
self-care

One of the biggest lessons I've learnt as I grow into a woman is that self-care isn't just about having facials and using scented candles. It's also about saying "no" when you need to protect your space, feeding your body with healthy food, taking responsibility for your actions, and forgiving yourself for what you could have done better in your past.

Self-care means different things to different people, and even your own perception of it can change depending on where you are on your life journey. So while my version is different to yours, the end goal should always be to care for yourself and offer yourself a love that no one else can give you.

At times, self-care means discipline, but it's also about letting go of limitations and learning to be free. My travels have contributed to my view of self-care because I've always had to adjust to new surroundings and people, and learn to make my own safe internal space. Without that sense of a safe space my mind can become dysfunctional, which influences my actions in all aspects of my life.

There are so many ways that you can incorporate self-care into your daily life. I always start my day by listening to some relaxing music while thanking the universe for another day.

This chapter shares different tips and tricks for creating your own self-care routine. I've found that mine is constantly evolving, depending on how I feel. But that's the fun part about it, so allow yourself to outgrow old habits with the intention of always loving who you are.

finding my self-care routine

Learning my self-care routine and watching it adapt according to where I am mentally or spiritually has been really insightful. My routine has helped me to balance my many different roles: entrepreneur, big sister, daughter, godmother, aunt, friend, employer, and employee. It's not easy, as I want to give each role 100 percent of my attention and energy, but I know it's easy to burn out when I try to do that, so being realistic and setting boundaries is important both for me and for others around me.

When my career took off I was at university, and there were so many times I wanted to quit to focus on building my online brand. But I knew the importance of not giving up, and I was able to prove to myself that I can achieve anything I put my mind to. The travels were fun on the outside, but in reality they affected the amount of energy I could give to my loved ones, and that made me feel very unbalanced.

Not that long ago I was addicted to working and had a hard time being still. My mind convinced me that if I wasn't working I must be wasting my time. It was the summer of 2017, and I'd traveled nonstop from March through to September. I found comfort in being away from home, but when I was back in my own space I didn't know how to be still. It was very hard for me to say "no" or to switch off.

When I returned from an eight-week trip around Africa I went through my first depression. It was really uncomfortable at first, as I couldn't quite put my finger on what was bothering me. I'd lost the ability to listen to my feelings as I was always on the move, always working. I felt burnt out and miserable, and I realized that something had to change.

It took a lot of unlearning bad habits to realize that I didn't always have to be doing something to be successful or feel fulfilled. We're not machines and we need quality time with ourselves to maintain stability. Stability is so important for our minds, and if we can't learn to be still with ourselves, we'll always be chasing something new to fill that space within.

I knew I had to find the things that could restore balance to my life. The first thing I did was spend more time with my brothers, running around with them in the park without wearing make-up or fancy clothes. I unleashed my inner child, and I felt free for the first time in a long time.

Now, my self-care routine depends on what I'm going through at that particular time. When I'm feeling emotionally drained, I always journal. If my mind is cluttered with my daily tasks, I'll clean my physical space in the hope that this will be reflected internally. Every Sunday I write a to-do list for the week ahead to help me stay organized.

Can you think of what would work for you?

create your self-care routine

Self-care is such an important part of maintaining a balanced life. We often get so caught up in the many roles that need our attention that we forget the person who's most deserving of it: ourselves. It can take time to find the right self-care routine, so begin by focusing on the small things that make you feel good and build from there.

My routine depends on my mood and how I feel in the moment. Some days this can inspire a big clean around my home. Decluttering my physical space inspires me to do the same internally. I find it therapeutic to watch a space transform from a mess into a calm and peaceful place. It feels like a reflection of the growth happening internally that I might not yet be able to see.

On days when I don't have much energy, binge-watching movies allows my mind to escape to a world of the unknown and can help my overthinking mind to press pause.

Self-care can never be found in a bottle or a cream. It's an abundance of things that make you feel good within. These may include the food you eat, your morning meditation ritual, dedicating time to read, or even putting your phone in flight mode for a few hours. Just find what works best for you.

my self-care list

When I've had a long or stressful day, I...

~ listen to Louise Hay affirmations

~ cook myself a healthy dinner

~ massage my face to release tension

~ binge-watch my favorite TV show

When I'm not feeling confident, I...

~ work out to release stress and empower myself

~ treat myself to a facial

~ repeat affirmations

~ listen to my favorite music

When I'm feeling demotivated or in a creative rut, I...

~ slow down and try to work out why I'm feeling this way

~ watch old content to remind myself of my abilities

~ look through photo albums to immerse myself in my previous travels

~ reflect on my achievements

When I'm feeling all over the place and unstable, I...

~ journal everything that's going on inside

~ clean my home

~ listen to music to clarify my thoughts

~ light candles and let the fragrances relax me

now it's your turn...

When I've had a long or stressful day, I…

....

....

....

....

When I'm feeling demotivated or in a creative rut, I…

....

....

....

....

....

....

When I'm not feeling confident, I…

....

....

....

....

When I'm feeling all over the place and unstable, I…

....

....

....

....

my self-care calendar

Mon	Tues	Wed	Thurs	Fri

Sat	Sun

Key

📱	24 hours without social media
🌹	Take myself on a date
🛋	Spend time with family
💆	Skincare pamper
▱	Meal preparation
📖	Reading time
👕	Donate old clothes
👟	Go for 20-minute jog
🍑x50	Complete 50 squats
🙏	Practice yoga
♡	One day serving others
🛌	Me time
👭	Spend time with friends
🧴	Deep condition hair
📖	Homework/study time
🧹	Monthly clean

my self-care journey

My self-care journey began when my relationship with my hair changed. I swapped the hours I'd previously spent on my hair, making it just right for the perfect selfie—hoping to attract an abundance of validation online—for time spent with my brothers, with my hair tied up in a bun. That shift influenced how I saw myself and how others saw me. I wanted to see myself for me and for others to do the same.

I was in Atlanta for an event, and I'd chosen to wear my hair tied up with a beautiful African print fabric. When I walked in, I went straight to the bathroom to check that I looked okay, and to build the courage I needed to be around everyone with such a different look. One of my friends affirmed that I looked just fine, so I went back out into the room. A short time later a woman approached me to take a picture. She looked at me boldly and said, "I'm so disappointed; we came all this way to see your hair."

Her words really affected me. I felt like I wasn't as worthy with my hair tied up as I was with it worn loose. Her words triggered my insecurity that I wasn't good enough without my hair. But I was working, and I had to keep my game face on and not let it affect me. When I returned to London, I focused my self-care routine on setting boundaries to live my life without wearing my hair as a safety blanket, or gain comfort from knowing it would grab the attention of others. I'd begun the journey of letting go.

It's easy to become comfortable or attached to something we know people will gravitate toward because, naturally, we like to be acknowledged and appreciated. We all want love and to feel affirmed by it, but the best acknowledgment you'll ever receive is the one from yourself. Knowing that you're beautiful with or without your attributes is your power.

After I cut my hair I took two weeks away from social media to spend quality time with myself. I knew I was in a vulnerable space and the words of others would impact me, so I wanted to affirm to myself that I was enough. I remember when I posted the first picture of my short hair. Some people were so upset—as if it was their own hair they'd cut that day—and others were so happy to see someone do something they wish they had the courage to do themselves.

I'd spent time investing in myself and empowering myself, so whether their words were good or bad, they didn't affect me because I knew I'd cut my hair only for myself. Now that my hair is growing, my relationship with it has changed. I have the confidence to go out with my hair tied back from my face, knowing that my aura will speak for itself.

It's hard to devote time to yourself when the influence of others can affect you heavily. When we place people too close to us their opinions can be seen as more important than our own. But the only person who will be truly affected by your actions of self-care is you.

Self-care is a journey,
not a destination.

tune in to your intuition

Have you noticed that sensation you get when something doesn't feel right?

Your intuition is powerful. Never ignore it. It will guide you through friendships, relationships, decisions, and confrontations.

It will guide you safely and in making the right decisions about your health.

Listen to your body when it tries to speak to you.

I never quite understood how to use the power of my intuition until I learnt how to sit still.

I want you to find a safe space in your home where you can sit for five to ten minutes.

When you find it, set the intention for your moment of stillness. I tend to focus on a sound or feeling, whether it's the sound of a clock ticking or the sensation of the soft rug beneath me.

Every time your mind wanders, thinking about the laundry you need to do or the assignment that's due, take yourself back to the sound or feeling.

Once you do this consistently, you'll be able to master resting your mind.

navigate your lows

Although I'm a very positive person, I also have moments of feeling low and it can be hard for me to step out of them. The biggest cause of my overthinking is fear and, naturally, as I get older I fear what my future holds and how the decisions I make now will impact who I become.

When I'm down I embrace every part of the pain, so that when it's time to let go I do it knowing that I'm not holding on to any unresolved problems that I didn't have the courage to face.

The first thing I do when I feel down is to push my ego to the side. When I've done that, I make sure I'm in a safe space where I can be free with my emotions. Then I ask myself what the problem is. Sometimes it's not easy to be open—you may be envious of someone, or not happy about where you are—because it will make you feel weak, but there's so much power in owning your lows in the same way that you own your highs.

Once you're aware of what's affecting you, the next step is to think about a solution. If there isn't one, then consider letting go of the problem, but if there's a solution then approach it with love and no expectation.

It's important to speak and listen to yourself whenever things don't feel right. Self-care is an abundance of beautiful things, but the most important for me is focusing on how my mind feels and what my soul needs.

Sometimes, when I get anxious or stressed, I need ideas to help me get out of my funk. I often find housework therapeutic, but when I don't have the energy for this I need to find something else. So, I made a little chart to help me find a self-care solution, and if you answer the questions you'll be able to find your solution too.

Self love is...
taking the time out
to find happiness.

Do you find peace in taking time to look after yourself?

No

Yes

Do you want to express your feelings but don't know how?

No

Treat yourself to a hot bath and mud mask night from time to time. Keep your phone turned off during these moments.

Yes

Do you like to be still and prefer to be in the moment?

No

Yes

Write about how you feel in a journal. You can either keep this to yourself or share it with someone to let them know how you're feeling.

Meditate for 20 minutes. You can choose to reflect on your day or enjoy the stillness.

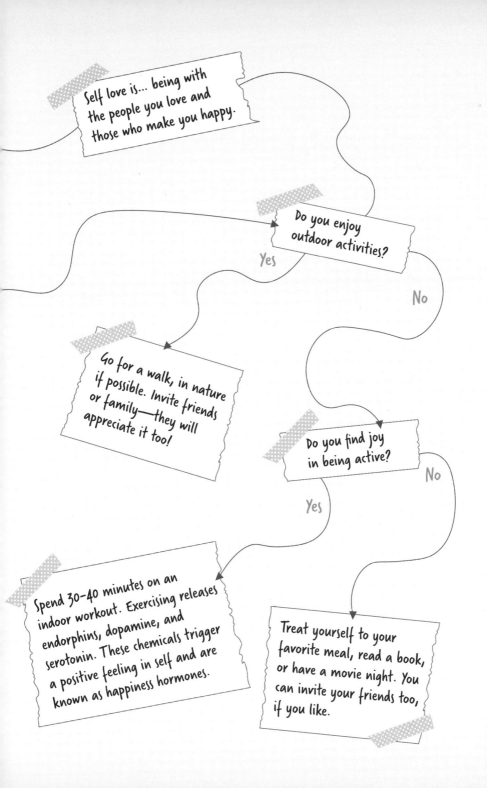

Self love is... being with the people you love and those who make you happy.

Do you enjoy outdoor activities?

Yes

No

Go for a walk, in nature if possible. Invite friends or family—they will appreciate it too!

Do you find joy in being active?

No

Yes

Spend 30-40 minutes on an indoor workout. Exercising releases endorphins, dopamine, and serotonin. These chemicals trigger a positive feeling in self and are known as happiness hormones.

Treat yourself to your favorite meal, read a book, or have a movie night. You can invite your friends too, if you like.

feel, heal, and grow

I'd rather give myself the best of me than invest my energy into others and then only have for myself what's left over. You can't expect others to give you the self-care only you know you deserve. The best part about this is that through every lesson you learn, you'll find new ways to care for yourself; every heartbreak and every scar on your skin have required healing. It's an evolving journey, so take the time to embrace that.

There are so many negative connotations around self-care equating to being selfish. I don't believe there's anything wrong with putting yourself first. For you to love others, you must be able to love yourself. For you to give to others, you must have already given to yourself. Setting those boundaries isn't easy, but it builds a strong foundation for you to know what you deserve in all aspects of your life.

Self-care is comforting, but it also requires discipline. If you have a goal in mind, focus on the goal rather than where you are now. Don't feel intimidated by the distance between where you are and where you need to go. It's easy to quit, but there's no reward for that. Go at your own pace, but don't get too comfortable. Some of my most rewarding experiences have been reaching goals that previously felt unachievable. Anything you want to do you can, as long as you believe in yourself.

Be transparent about your self-care journey with those around you. They're more likely to support you, and might even feel inspired and join you on the journey. Whenever I'm going through a transition of self-care, whether it's working on internal healing or having moments of solitude to realign myself, I'm always honest about it with the people around me so they don't take my distance personally. I appreciate these moments, even when they're uncomfortable, because they allow me to speak my truth.

I like to look at anything I want to let go of as a challenge that takes me to another level. Just like a form of fitness or embarking on a new activity, the more you practice, the stronger you become. Whenever I have a moment of healing, I know that I'm letting go of something to enable a door to open to something new. Life brings you things at the time you need them, but you have to trust the process and not question it. Sometimes I've only seen the impact of my self-care practice months later, when it was revealed to me through a person or an experience. So, allow yourself to feel, heal, and grow. You should never want to stay in the same place mentally, physically, or spiritually, knowing that you can be elevated to being an even better version of yourself than you are now.

chapter 3
body

A body. We all have one.

Curvy, slim, round, tall, **short**, or **strong**, but most importantly **BEAUTIFUL**.

One of the most wonderful things about being a woman is that we come in many different shapes and sizes, and we should all embrace that. It's an empowering moment when you realize that your body is far more than its physical attributes, and it has the ability to help you heal, grow, and move through life.

It took me a while to love my body, as I was so fixated on the idea of wanting to have more. The idea of having more curves, a bigger booty, bigger boobs, longer legs, a slimmer waist, and a perfect hourglass shape convinced me to believe that I wasn't enough without those things.

What I discovered when I was looking for more was that I stopped embracing and enjoying what I have now. Instead of acknowledging how amazing my body is, I was always looking for flaws to dwell on and things to fix. I don't want to look back at pictures of my body and regret that I didn't embrace it. It's time to learn to love what we have now before we regret it later.

This chapter is inspired by all the women who own everything about their body and choose to love it. You rock!

my journey of acceptance

I love being both Zimbabwean and English. When I'm around women from both cultures, I'm reminded of how different we all are, but also how that should be embraced and not looked down upon. My relationship with my body has been a journey of acceptance.

I've always been slim, and that was a topic of conversation at family gatherings. My weight was questioned and this brought me down a lot—I felt like I wasn't enough and didn't have the body shape of a typical Zimbabwean woman. But I'm not a typical woman. I'm Nia, and all I am is enough. As I grew through puberty my body shape changed but I still kept my slim figure. When I realized that I couldn't change my body, but I could tone and strengthen it, I decided to change how I saw it.

Whenever I've been sick or stressed, I've seen the true strength of my body and its journey of healing. The mind is a powerful place, but watching a scar heal or a bone repair itself always reminds me that everything will get better with time, and I just need to be patient. I broke my arm when I was ten, and for six weeks I couldn't use it. It was the arm I wrote with too, which created an even bigger challenge. This made me appreciate what it is to write without wearing a cast or a sling, and to be able to raise my hands without my arm falling because the bones weren't strong enough to hold them. I had to break my arm to appreciate it and all the things it does for me when I should have already appreciated it.

Now I'm in a space where I love my body. I no longer wish for things to be added or modified, but am grateful for it every day. No matter what I'm doing, I know I have the ability to do it through my body. I'm far more than the dip on my hip or the small pouch on my stomach that reminds me of womanhood.

I'm strength whenever I overcome sickness. I'm confidence whenever I stride into a room. I'm freedom whenever I play in a garden with my brothers. I'm joy whenever I dance at a party. It's time to change the narrative of what our bodies look like and instead focus on what they can do. It's time to stop comparing our bodies to someone else's, and instead to love the one that we wake up in everyday.

I want you to think of all the amazing things your body can do, and appreciate that it will always be there to comfort you and nurture you, no matter what. It will grow as you do and it will heal with you. It's been with you this far and it still has a long way to go, so be gentle and be kind. The words you use to describe it are powerful, so affirm its beauty and embrace its strength.

appreciate your body

A woman's journey of body confidence changes constantly throughout her life. My relationship with my body began at a young age, as my lack of weight was always a topic of conversation at family gatherings. There was the stereotypical assumption that a skinny body wasn't a healthy one, even though it was my high metabolism that stopped me from putting on weight.

I focused on my skin to divert my attention from the rest of my body. I almost neglected my physical health, knowing that I could eat whatever I wanted without putting on weight, and didn't need to work out to keep my weight stable. That narrative changed when I turned 21 and my metabolism slowed down; it forced me to focus on my body's health.

There are so many strong women around me who have broken bones, worked in tough conditions, fought cancer, created and carried life for nine months, and healed from abuse. These women have always risen to the challenges that life has presented them, and allowed their bodies to guide them through their journey.

That ability is to be celebrated. Your body needs to be acknowledged for its daily commute to work, its determination to push through a workout, its ability to bring and nurture life, and even its ability to protect you from danger.

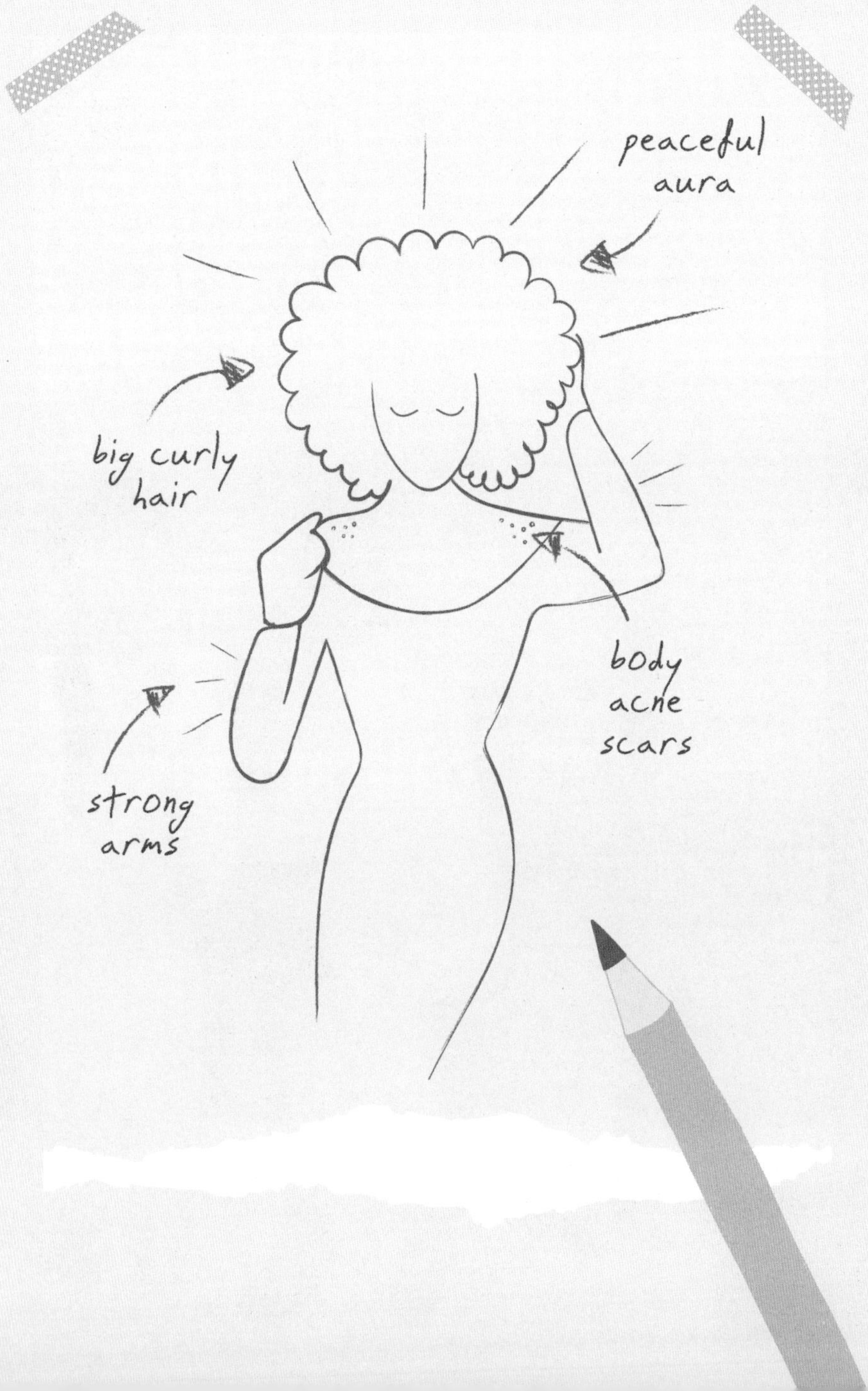
peaceful aura
big curly hair
body acne scars
strong arms

body image

It's amazing how our minds can hinder how we see ourselves. When I was about fifteen, I went to a workshop at which we were asked to draw ourselves from different perspectives—a bird's eye view, another with our eyes closed, and a third without removing the pen from the paper. It was so fun to see how carefree I could be when I didn't overthink so much.

Back then, if I had twenty minutes to draw myself freely, I probably would have drawn how I thought my body looked rather than how it *actually* looked. I probably wouldn't have highlighted the flaws, but tried to edit them to make myself feel better. I probably would have strived for perfection that didn't exist.

I want you to try drawing yourself without taking your pen off the paper. Let your hands be free and see what you create. Try not to be a perfectionist but to accept what is.

Did you notice how you felt when you drew certain parts of your body? Self-love is a journey not a destination, and the journey of loving your body is the same, too. It's always changing and so is the way we see ourselves.

Look in the mirror and speak to your body. Thank it for everything it does for you, and also compliment it for all the things you love about it. Apologize for any things you find yourself criticizing. Do this every morning and night or every time you look in the mirror, and watch how your energy changes.

perfectly flawed

I used to suffer from acne. Although it affected my skin, I also allowed it to affect my mind. I hid behind my hair in the hope that no one would notice the skin I was ashamed of. I covered myself in make-up with the intention of being perfect. I always believed that once my skin cleared up I'd become more confident, but instead, when my skin cleared I searched for more flaws on which to focus my attention.

When the acne on my face cleared, my back began to develop its own consistent breakouts. The way I saw myself and the narrative I had within was negative, so of course nothing ever got better. For so long we've attached our worth to the way we look, but trying to be different doesn't make anyone less of a person. Instead, we become less of a person when we try to be anything but ourselves.

We've been taught to fix our flaws, yet nothing about you is broken, Queen. I love the lines of love that grow on my thighs and remind me of my journey from girl to woman. I love the scars on my back that remind me to be careful about the food I eat and to take greater care of the way I treat my skin.

Don't try to rush Mother Nature. You'll bloom just the way you're supposed to, when you're supposed to. Embrace who you are now, as the person you'll be isn't here yet.

Love those rolls and love that skin. Let your soul shine from within.

lists of love

I want you to think about what you love about your body and what you don't love. More importantly, I want you to understand why. Is the idea of not being good enough, or perhaps a comment that someone made, affecting how you see yourself? It's time to let go of those ideas, and move the things you don't love to the never-ending list of the things you do love.

Write five things you love about your body, and why.

....

....

....

....

....

Write five things you don't love about your body, and why.

....

....

....

....

....

My body is

....
....
....
....

I love the...

....
....
....
....
....

of my body

Things I'll learn to love about my body are

....
....
....
....

My body can

....
....
....
....
....

My favorite part of my body is

....
....
....

I love the way it curves,
I love the way it heals,
I love the way it feels.
I love my body.

trust your body

I love being a woman and I love looking at pictures to see how I've evolved to become one. I've come to understand that everything happens in stages, and each stage isn't to be rushed but to be felt. In the same way that you can't rush the growth of a flower, you can't rush your body.

A woman's body is truly amazing, and I'll never take for granted the opportunities I have to use it to learn new things. As a kid I was always adventurous—I took dance classes and learnt how to ice skate—and my body never let me down, no matter what I tried. Now that I'm a woman, I find that fear can sometimes hold me back and stop me from letting go and being free. I recently bought skates with my best friend as the idea of learning this skill was amazing, but when I tried it I was scared of falling. I was scared of scarring my skin or hurting myself.

Then I realized that even if I did fall, my bruises would soon fade, and I found the courage I needed to try something that was new and unfamiliar. Don't let fear stop you from letting yourself go and trying new things. Enroll in that yoga class and watch how you improve each session, or try skiing and see how you glide across the snow with grace and confidence.

My body plays a big part in my self-care routine. It sets the tone for how I see myself, and I value quality time with myself to focus on that. It's important to have a self-care routine so you know how to reset and refresh. Recently, I've had to immerse myself in my routine because even though my body is strong, I'll lose that strength if I don't take good care of it. I have a bad habit of being so focused on work that I forget to eat, but if I'm not at my best then how will my work be? Having this mindset has given me the discipline to work and to take the breaks I need.

It's important to know when to be still and nurture your body. You only have one, and you should cherish it and care for it. Whenever I feel run down, I always listen to my body and it never leads me in the wrong direction. So when my stomach cramps, I know Mother Nature is on her way, or when I have a headache, I know it's time to put work aside and be still for a moment. Whenever I'm in fear, I trust that my body will give me the energy to act accordingly.

Trust that your body will always be there through every part of your journey. Listen to it and protect it. Remember that it isn't unproductive to rest or to focus on the health of your body internally. Doing so allows you to strengthen so that you can pick yourself up from feeling down.

thank your body

When we think of our body, the first thing we think of are the physical qualities it gives us. Imagine the abundance of joy we'd feel by appreciating all the things our body does for us each day, from the way our toes give us balance on our journey, to the way our back carries our weight. No matter how big or small, every part of us contributes to how we move through life.

My hands are one of my favorite things about my body. They're involved in everything I do, from cleaning my home and creating a safe space to recording the ideas I have or the projects I want to be a part of. My hands are vessels for me to express everything that's in my mind.

Every time I travel, I appreciate my body even more. The way it adjusts to different climates and time zones, all to help me fully experience the beauty of the country I'm visiting, is amazing to me. I remember when I went backpacking in India, and I carried everything in one bag. At times it was so frustrating and tiring, but my body always pushed through no matter how drained I was.

I want you to think of your favorite part of your body, and about all the amazing things it does for you every day. If it's your hands or feet then show your appreciation with a massage, or if it's your stomach then feed it with something delicious and healthy. Your body will thank you for it.

celebrate your body

When I was 18 I took part in a pageant. It was a really insightful part of my journey because it taught me that every woman who stood on stage with me deserved to win, and we were all beautiful. We all had our own things that made us special and unique.

We were judged on our compassion, on how we might use the title to create positive change, on our talents, the way we walked, and how nice our dresses looked. We weren't judged on our triumphs, the things we'd overcome in our lives, or our journeys as women.

We're more than just the clothing we wear or the skills we possess. We're an abundance of so many things, including the times when the only option we had was to rise above pain, and the times when we shone from doing what we love. We all deserve to be celebrated.

What do you want to start celebrating about yourself?

love your body

The most beautiful thing about a woman's body is that it will always change, just like you. It will stretch when you grow from girl to woman— it will curve, it will soften, it will strengthen, and it will elongate. The most important part of that journey is to love where you are at each stage. Every cycle of a woman's life from puberty to menopause should be celebrated. Embrace where you are now, Queen.

Speak to your body with kindness, love it the best way you know how, nurture it with joy and richness, nourish it with healing foods, comfort it during hard times, and embrace it for being amazing. The longest relationship you'll ever have is the one with yourself, so make sure you love it and cherish it.

Start your day by appreciating what's in front of you rather than wishing for what only exists in your mind. You're beautiful just the way you are, and knowing this is your power. You're not defined by the way your cellulite shows when you dance, or by the way your stomach rolls when you're cozy in bed. All of these things make you the goddess you are.

Remember that you're not less of a woman if flaunting your body gives you joy, or if covering it brings you peace. It's your body, and the rules and boundaries you create with it deserve to be acknowledged and respected. Never let anyone tell you what you can and can't do with your body based on their expectations of a woman. You set your own expectations and you create our own boundaries.

Since I began embracing all of the tremendous things my body does for me, I've found that my relationship with it has changed. It's so much more than just its physical attributes—it's my safe space, it's my companion during my adventures, it's my guide during moments of panic, it's my blanket when I'm cold, it's my intuition during times of confusion, and it's mine.

Instead of focusing on the things I don't have, I express gratitude for the things I do. I have beautiful long legs that take me anywhere I want to go. I have shoulders that carry my equipment to create, even when the day is long. I have hands that can transform an outfit or cook a meal that gives people joy. I have a stomach that's the best place to hold whenever I crave comfort.

It's important to recognize what your body does for you and all the things you can do for it. Can you invest time in the gym to tone up or release stress? Can you eat healthier meals to keep you active in your daily life? Can you treat yourself to a massage when you start to feel tense? Or can you exfoliate your skin in the shower to give yourself a fresh start?

Find your own unique way to love your body and in return it will love you back.

lines of love

Lines of love,
scars with a story.

The beauty of a woman comes from within, and I think the most important thing a woman can do is own every part of herself. I'm inspired by how our skin can tell a story and emphasize the strength we possess, the challenges we've overcome, and the growth we've achieved.

This part of the book shares the journey of women just like you and me who have accepted parts of their body and skin that form part of their story. We all have something we stare at in the mirror, or fantasize about, wondering what life would be like without it. But this is what makes you who you are. Own it and embrace it.

I have a family of beautiful and amazing souls who have followed me on my social journey and I wanted them to be a part of this book too. Last year, I wrote a message on my channels to see who would want to be a part of this project, and these beautiful women shared the most incredible stories. As I was reading them I realized how I could relate to each and every woman, which was so powerful and extraordinary. I used their words the best way I knew how—to inspire illustrations that reflect their lines of love and scars with a story.

I hope they inspire you to see yourself as art, as beautiful and as you. Thank you to all the phenomenal women who were brave enough to speak their truth; you've inspired me to live with the freedom and self-acceptance that you do. This is my gift to you.

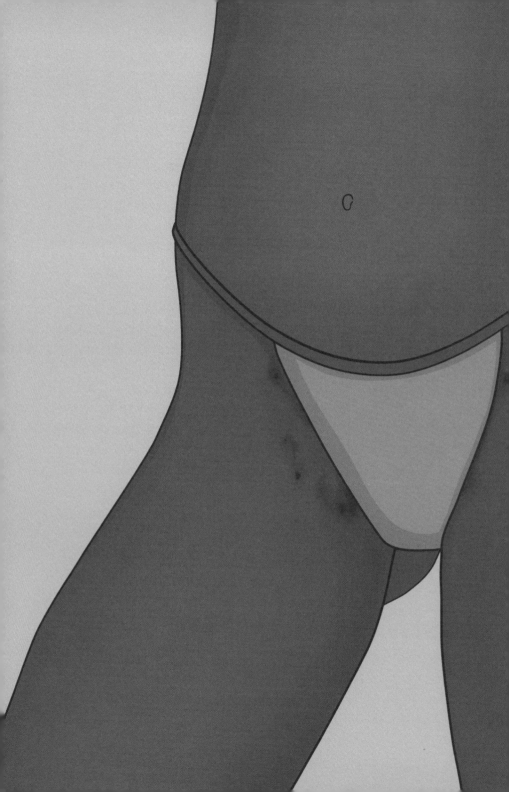

nia's story

I started waxing when I was seventeen years old. I've always been self-conscious of my hair, from the big curls that grow on my head to the tufts of hair on my legs.

My desire to have smooth skin started at a young age. I watched adverts of women having their legs waxed with strips and thought that sanitary pads would do the same thing. Now this makes me laugh. I'm lucky enough to be able to afford the upkeep of the things that make me feel most confident, yet I've been left with the scars from all my different experiments.

I remember a photoshoot in New York City which required me to wear a bodysuit. I had to tell the photographer that I wouldn't be able to shoot because I had scars. I was always apologizing to people for my scars or any hair that made me feel uncomfortable.

It wasn't until I was booked for a campaign with Aerie, a company that empowers women by showing natural and raw images of their models, that things really changed. When I arrived on set, the make-up artists told me to stop apologizing for my scars as I'd soon be flaunting them to the world on a Times Square billboard. I'll never forget the moment I saw myself on that billboard. I knew that my inner child was jumping up and down as I'd finally set myself free by allowing my scars to be seen by the entire world.

I no longer apologize to anyone on behalf of my body.

zoe's story

I first noticed my scarring after suffering from acne. I was sixteen, and going through a traumatic experience which led me to develop anxiety, OCD, and dermatillomania (a skin-picking condition linked to OCD). I guess I started to focus on my appearance as a distraction, and my main focus was my skin.

I tried to treat my acne by spending endless amounts of money on anti-acne products, scar treatments, facials, and even acid peels. I used make-up to cover my scars, and for years I didn't go swimming or wear vest tops because of the scars on my chest and back. When I was pregnant I went on holiday to Greece, and I just decided it was "now or never." It hit me that after this I'd be holidaying with a baby and something just clicked—I realized my time to feel free wasn't "next time" but now!

After giving birth to my son, I truly learnt to love my scarring. In the weeks before his birth, I'd been disappointed when my skin began to ripple and stretch. My labor was tough and doctors feared for my son's life, but when he was born I was just so grateful that this body of mine had made such a perfect, healthy baby. In that moment, my scars—in particular my stretch marks—were signs of strength, growth, and life.

Now I know that my beauty comes from the words I speak, how I interact with others, the good things I do for people, how I love my son, and how I love God. Beauty is my spirit.

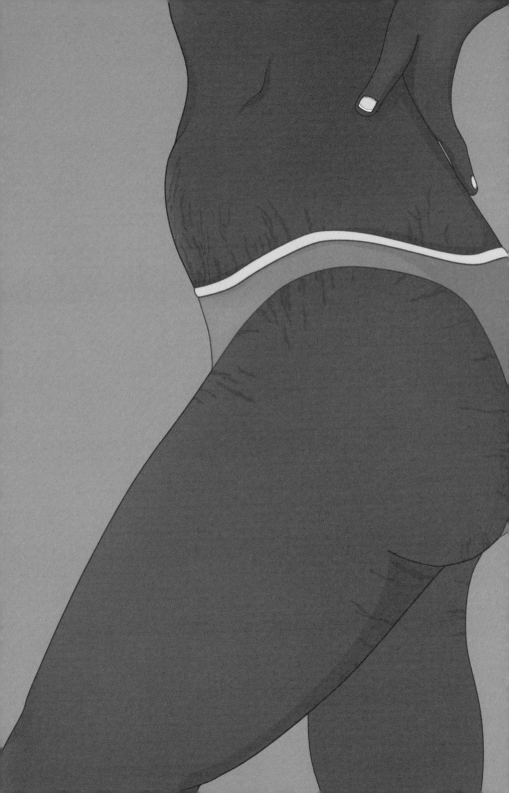

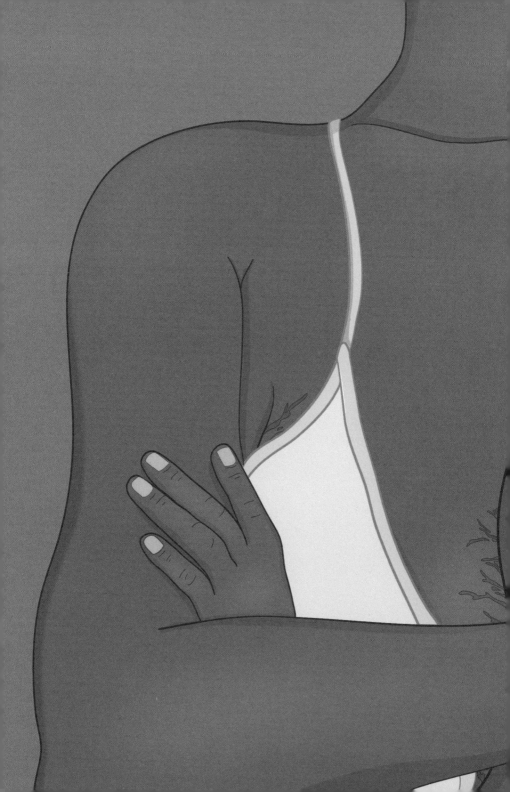

maja's story

I first noticed my scarring when I was about twelve. Stretch marks began to appear across my chest, which made me feel insecure and affected my self-esteem. I felt self-conscious whenever I wore scoop-neck tops because I thought everyone (especially boys) would look at my chest and see these ugly lines that you only get if you're pregnant or really overweight.

After researching online, I came to the conclusion that I was just fat and began to hate my body for creating these ugly marks. I spent hours reading about creams, home remedies, and "miracle" products to get rid of stretch marks. When they didn't work I just covered up my body.

That's now in the past. I learnt to love my scarring after seeing other women who had stretch marks but didn't care. Social media allowed me to realize that stretch marks are beautiful. I'm still learning to love mine everyday, but what helps is listening to Kendrick Lamar's *Humble* – he even celebrates stretch marks!

For me, my beauty comes from my ancestors. I'm sure the women in my family have had stretch marks for generations and not cared about how other people might judge them. They had more important things to worry about, like raising capable children who would go on to thrive for generations. How silly of me to worry about what strangers think of me when my ancestors worked so hard for me to be where I am today.

sukayna's story

I remember the times when my cousins and I went to parties wearing spaghetti-strap dresses, but an auntie or grown-up would say to me: "Get a scarf or a cardigan to cover your back," because I had acne and scars on it. So I started covering up and started buying products to help get rid of the acne. I tried everything I could, but it was as if the acne and scars were saying, "We're with you for life, so stop trying to get rid of us."

When I was eighteen I went to university in Switzerland. A few months later I met a women who had all the flaws I had, but she was on the beach, her skin shimmering with cocoa butter, without a care in the world. I remember sitting there and saying to myself: *One day I want to be just like that woman.*

I guess sometimes you speak things into existence. Slowly, I began trying to block thoughts and care less about what people and society might think about me. I focused all my energy on making myself better. Then I started looking for people who motivated or inspired me, and soon I found Nia!

Today, I still have scars and stretch marks, but I've found the confidence to own my flaws by surrounding myself with the right energy, getting inspired by the right people and, of course, changing my mindset.

I feel that my beauty comes from within, from my visions of positive change, from the happiness I feel, and from the energy with which I fill myself.

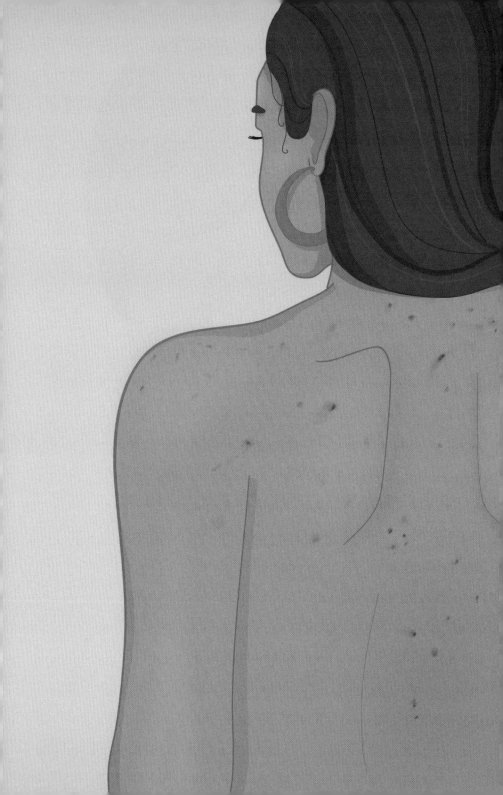

armani's story

I first saw my C-section scar in the hospital, two days after the birth of my daughter. In order to be discharged with my baby, I had to get up, remove the dressing from my C-section wound, and shower by myself. So, that day in the shower, I looked down at the scar and realized my abdomen would never be the same again.

I was most self-conscious about my scar when I was with a lover. I dreaded baring myself to them. The result of the most beautiful experience in the world made me feel the most self-conscious. I began loving my scar a couple years ago, after embarking on a journey of self-love. I had to love myself because I was tired of expecting men to, and because I needed to teach my daughter to do the same. And she'll do what I do before she does what I ask.

My beauty comes from my intelligence, from the way my mind works, and from the hard work I put in as a single mom to earn my degree. My beauty comes from my blackness, and from my journey to accepting myself in a world that values whiteness. My beauty comes from being a mother, a creator of life.

I've learnt that my deep self-confidence issues resulted in me giving my body away to people who didn't love me. As a result of that triumph and pain I know that I'm stronger and wiser, I'm beautiful, and my opinion of myself is all that matters.

mercy's story

I was burnt when I was around two or three years old. I was running around the house wearing my favorite purple sweater, and when I ran into the kitchen I slipped and knocked over a pot of boiling water, which spilled onto my body. In a panic, the hot sweater was ripped from me and this ended up causing my scarring. The shock to my body was so intense that it triggered laughter instead of screaming.

I was in and out of reconstructive surgery for years after the incident. My final surgery required a skin graft, but my parents didn't want to create more scars so they left my skin to heal as it was. I kept asking them to allow me to have the final surgery, but they told me that the decision would be mine once I was older.

I can't pinpoint that "aha" moment that transformed my life. When I was younger I used to cry over everything, but once I learnt to process my emotions I realized how unique my scar made me. Later, I began noticing how my complexion and my smile also made me unique, and that I had other unique features too. I was radiating confidence and receiving so much love from others who could feel it.

Instead of feeling uncomfortable around people who don't share similarities with me, I see it as something that makes me stand out. Individuality is such a powerful thing. I love this about people and the beauty that's attached to it.

chapter 4
relationships

Love is the most beautiful thing that souls can share with each other. I've learnt so much about myself from relationships. I've discovered how caring I can be, how strong I am, and how empowering it can be to love another soul. I've learnt about my own vulnerability and sensitivity, embracing every part of it. There's so much power in owning all the things you've grown through and realizing that your strength is admirable; it's all a part of your story. Don't let one bad chapter hinder the rest of your book!

Love can also be the most transformative experience of your life. I've left each of my relationships feeling different to the girl I was at the beginning. Sometimes it hurts to let go, but we don't have possession of anyone in this lifetime; we just have memories to create and lessons to learn. So give yourself the permission and freedom to love without holding on too tight to something that may not serve you.

I love love. It comes in many different forms, but the feeling is always the same. The core of all those forms starts with you.

This chapter will highlight the beauty of being with and loved by someone, but also of being present and loved by yourself. It will dive into a variety of relationships that you can experience—relationships between parents and children, friends and foes, boyfriends and girlfriends—showing that there's so much love to embrace and enjoy in every different aspect of life.

love, love, love

This is probably the most vulnerable topic in this journal of mine and yours, as love is something we can't live without. Although I'm still young, I've had a lot of experience with unhealthy relationships with both friends and lovers. But the lessons I've learnt from them have strengthened me in ways I couldn't have imagined. I look at all the relationships I've had as lessons or blessings (ultimately the lessons are blessings too). We don't have possession over anyone on this Earth, just some time to make memories in.

The biggest lesson I've learnt from my relationships has been to be conscious of the one you have with yourself. Before I worked on my relationship with myself, I depended on my friends for validation, and when they didn't reciprocate that energy I felt rejected. We have friends for different reasons, and it's better to accept them as they are instead of layering your expectations onto them.

We have some friends we can call at 3 a.m. when something is wrong and they'll pick up, we have friends we can cry with, some we can dance the night away with, and some we can just be still with. You can find those qualities in one person or in many different people.

Whenever people enter our lives, they're a mirror of who we are or what we need at that moment in time. Sometimes, they remind us of a lesson we need to learn or something we need to let go of. I used to find that if I wasn't learning the lesson then the same type of person kept appearing in my life. They felt familiar or had the same characteristics as another and I didn't understand why. Then I realized I was attracting them because I needed to let go of pain and trauma that I hadn't acknowledged. When my life was hectic and busy with no sense of stability, I found that I attracted people who calmed me down or allowed me to be still. When I was getting too comfortable, I found that I attracted people who would push me to be better and want more for myself.

Think about the people you have in your life right now and what you have learnt from them so far. Sometimes the learning doesn't happen until you go on your own journey, and that's fine. Think of everyone in your life—family, friends, lovers—then really consider your relationship and how healthy it is. This should allow you to see where you are mentally and why these people are around you.

Whenever I think of the toxic relationships I've been in, I wonder why I didn't have the strength to leave or why I felt that I deserved to be disrespected. And although those experiences were uncomfortable, they set the tone for my relationships now.

You deserve more than to be in a relationship that makes you feel unworthy or brings you down. You deserve to be in a relationship that celebrates you. You deserve to be in a relationship that empowers you to be an even better version of yourself, to be in a relationship in which you can create positive memories and grow together.

allow your soul to bloom

In a garden, all flowers bloom in their own time.

Once I learnt that this applies to the women I surround myself with, I became confident about the time it's taken for my soul to bloom.

Sometimes it's easy to compare yourself to others, but never forget to acknowledge your journey and achievements.

There's so much more power and strength when women unite because, just like the flowers in a garden, we all possess so many beautiful characteristics which are truly enhanced when we stand among each other.

And just like flowers, we all have our own color, shape, size, and unique flare.

Let go of the idea that we must compete with each other to be the best version of ourselves. There's enough room in the garden for us all to blossom.

Choose to lift up the women in your life and watch your garden bloom.

lessons in love

Some of my most beautiful lessons were learnt from my most painful experiences.

Through relationships I've learnt how powerful I can be, how caring I am, and how I want to be loved.

Whatever you desire in a relationship you must be able give to yourself. If you don't love yourself, how can you expect anyone to love you?

All relationships you go through are for you to grow *through*.

I want you to reflect on your past relationships–the ones that made you laugh, the ones that made you cry, and the ones that contributed to who you are now. Write about your lessons in love opposite or in your journal.

Some relationships may not have ended how you imagined, but you have shared memories and the good ones will always be there for you to revisit. The bad ones are there for you to heal from.

Make peace with them for they made you into the strong, vulnerable, sensitive, and amazing woman you are.

What did your last relationship teach you?

....

....

....

....

What was your favorite memory in that relationship?

....

....

....

....

....

What did you learn about yourself?

....

....

....

What is something you want to tell your last love?

....

....

....

....

grow through your relationships

Love comes in many different forms and it's one of the most beautiful feelings I've experienced. Each soul in my life has taught me something new to elevate me in ways I might not have otherwise achieved. I've learnt to be more adventurous through a lover who loved to see the world; I've learnt to be more calm thanks to a lover who liked to be still and take things as they come; and I've felt empowered by a lover who was attracted to my ambition.

I've met love in some pure forms, but I've also met it at its darkest and most toxic. I've learnt that how a person treats you depends not only on how they feel about you, but more importantly how they feel about themselves.

One particular relationship taught me more than the others. I rebelled against what was expected. His manipulation taught me about my own boundaries. His entitlement taught me about putting myself first. His control emboldened my free spirit. And now, looking back, if I'd never experienced that relationship I wouldn't know what I truly deserve.

The hardest part about being in a relationship isn't knowing when to let go, it's letting go of the idea of who that person could be. You need to give yourself the advice you'd give a friend if they told you your story. Would you tell them to stay with someone who doesn't enhance their radiance? Or would you encourage them to heal and guide them through that journey?

When people talk about love they say it isn't easy, but they never say it's hard.

your relationships

It's important to manifest your goals and achievements, but you should also manifest the kind of relationship you want to be in. Do you want a relationship that excites you, empowers you, or makes you feel safe? It's also okay if you don't want to be with a partner. How you feel is important, Queen. Never forget that.

What kind of relationship do you want to be in?

....

....

....

I want to be a lover who...

....

....

....

....

How do I want to feel when I'm with my partner?

....

....

....

....

....

....

....

What kind of memories do I want to create?

....

....

....

My dream partner will make me feel...

....

....

....

....

....

....

Qualities that I want my partner to have are...

....

....

....

What do I need to heal from in order to be the best partner I can be?

....

....

....

I will not be
loved in parts
as I was not
made in pieces.

the beauty of friendship

One of the most beautiful blessings in life is friendship. I've been lucky to attract an abundance of friends over the years. The beauty of life is that we're always growing, but sadly some people don't quite grow in alignment with you. Writing this page was a little hard for me as I had to reflect on people who are no longer in my life. It made me see how my actions might have impacted where we are today, and yet that reflection allowed me to acknowledge how important those people were in my development.

My first lesson in friendship came when I was five years old. I'd just started school, and everyone except one girl in my class made it apparent that I was different. She never questioned who I was. She'd had a tough upbringing, so my mum would always invite her over for home-cooked meals or she'd come on day trips with my family. When we ended up going to different high schools we lost touch, but that friendship taught me to accept people as they are, to accept them as they show up.

I had another friend who I was shoulder to shoulder with as we grew up. We were both quiet, but when we went to each other's house we'd play our favorite songs and practice our catwalks. She was the most significant friend I had, and she taught me what it meant to be a true friend. When I began building a brand I allowed that work to swallow up the time I'd previously devoted to her, and we drifted apart. We never took the time to express our feelings, and instead let pride get in the way. That friendship taught me to communicate even when it's uncomfortable, and it taught me about sisterhood and how to balance time between work and the people you love.

I had a friend who was always up to mischief; she brought out both my adventurous and sheltered sides. We had sleepovers night after night and spent so much quality time together; I felt like we were family. We had fun, but when I reached my limit of fun she thought I was being boring so I distanced myself. That friendship taught me how to set boundaries and how to say 'no.'

Later, I had a friend who shared the same career ambitions. She taught me how to explore my creativity and experiment with style. We shared so many beautiful memories which were a huge part of my journey to womanhood. But the love for our careers suffocated our friendship and business got in the way. When things fell apart, my judgment of her actions blocked my ability to forgive her. That friendship taught me that we all make mistakes and forgiveness can bring release from pain.

Friends are just as important as lovers, and it's such a beautiful feeling to build that sense of sisterhood with someone so different from yourself. I'm learning to let go and allow people to flow out of my life as smoothly as they entered it. We have no possession over anyone in this lifetime. Some people have a message to give to you, but once their time is up let them go. If they're meant to be in your life, they'll always come back.

sisterhood

Which kind of friend do you want to be?

....

....

....

....

....

What kind of friend are you?

....

....

....

....

What have you learnt from your friendships so far?

....

....

....

What do you love about your friends?

....

....

....

....

....

What do you want to work on within your friendships?

....

....

....

acknowledge the women before you

To all the women before us—the mothers, grandmothers, aunties, and big sisters—who've created spaces that enable us to move freely through life, I give thanks.

I'm grateful to my mum for sharing her wisdom and strength. She's a great example of how to move through life with understanding and compassion. She taught me all about strength, even when I'm at my weakest. She also encouraged me to travel, and her photo albums of memories around the world inspired me to create my own. I'm also grateful for how much my mum taught me about my culture. One of my favorite childhood memories is being carried on her back wrapped in a gumbeze (a blanket) while she cooked or cleaned. That bond is something I'll always cherish.

I remember being on set for a really big brand. While I waited to be called, I thought of a girl landing in London to begin her journey in a part of the world she was yet to discover. That girl was my mum. I don't know whether she ever daydreamed about what her daughter would be like, but I knew on set that day that I was making a lot of women before me feel proud.

You're already opening doors for future female leaders, philanthropists, politicians, doctors, creatives, models, scientists, engineers, authors, and more, and that's something to be proud of and to own in every action you make.

give love, receive love

It's time to fall in love with yourself, Queen. It's time to fall in love with your flaws, to fall in love with the beautiful lines of love that form on your skin as it stretches to remind you of your superpowers. It's time to fall in love with the way your mind evolves through the lessons that become blessings, to fall in love with the way you smile when you talk about your dreams, and to fall in love with your soul—even the deep, dark corners that reveal your hidden secrets. Most importantly, it's time to fall in love with yourself before you allow anyone else to. It's time to fall in love with you, Queen. All the experiences I grew through inspired me to love the woman I am today.

The friendships I had to let go taught me that I'm my greatest friend. The relationships that didn't turn out quite how I imagined taught me that only I can truly love myself the way I want to be loved, and that love is something beautiful I deserve to feel and experience. They taught me not to have expectations or to create a version of someone who doesn't exist. It's important not to fall in love with the idea of someone, but to fall in love with them and then create the idea. The energy I choose to surround myself with has the power to uplift me or bring me down.

Despite my many relationships with others, the most important one I have is with myself. This sets the tone for how everyone else treats me.

Never betray yourself for a friendship that no longer serves you, or a relationship that only seems to drain you. Everyone has their time with you; some relationships may be short and others may be long, but don't try to force a relationship to continue when it's simply ended.

This has been the toughest part of my journey to understand and let go of, but the feeling of clearing out space following the departure of those who taught me what I needed to learn is so good for the soul.

Love is a beautiful part of our lives. It should be felt with joy, passion, excitement, adventure, peace, and fulfillment. In every relationship in my life—with family, friends, and lovers—I set the intention to receive love and give love. I'm worthy of this and so are you.

Never settle for a relationship just to feel full if you're being served something empty.

I'm so proud of myself for everything I've achieved and everything that I will achieve. Isn't it incredible how we're able to learn new things and discover our passion through life's experiences? Some of my best projects began when I was feeling low and needed an outlet to express my creativity, or when I was feeling lonely and wanted something to focus my mind on.

Since I was young, my dream job has changed so many times. When I saw that curly hair was cool, I wanted to be a singer like Scary Spice. Then, thanks to school discos, I wanted to dance like Beyoncé. On my first trip to the USA with my mum I dreamt of being a flight attendant so I could see the world. Then, when I spent all day sketching clothes I wished I could wear, I told the whole world I'd be a fashion designer. During university, I wanted to be a journalist so I could capture the stories of the world and shed light on topics that weren't being discussed. As I've grown and evolved, so have my dreams. You can be whatever you want to be and it's never too late to chase those dreams. Don't chase your parents' goals, your friends', or your teachers'—chase yours!

You have the ability to do whatever you dream of, but passion is the first thing that will lead you in the right direction. I've found that the most successful people are never driven by money but by creating change in the world. This same drive is what keeps you focused and motivated through the hiccups that come with running a business.

girl boss

I still feel overwhelmed when I reflect on my journey and how I was able to build my empire at such a young age. Many people ask me how I did it, and my first answer is that I believed I could achieve my dreams. You can, too. Just don't let fear stop you from achieving them.

When I was 16, I decided to create an Instagram account to document my life as a teenager in London. It was a creative outlet to express my love of hair, fashion, and having fun with my friends. My mum worked hard to make sure I had the essential items I needed, but I didn't shop in the "new arrivals" sections of stores; instead you'd find me looking for gems on the sale rails at the back of the shop. I learnt to make use of what I had, and that attitude helped to prepare me for this industry. It taught me that you can make something out of nothing, and I always try to remember that when the pressures of having it all overwhelm me.

I've always been big on friendships. I grew up watching my mum overextend herself for the people around her, and my association with strong friendships stems from that. As a teenager I had three groups of friends who were very different. It was important that I could be myself in each group as I knew I could be taken off my path by trying to fit in.

The fear of getting into trouble kept me in my bedroom on my laptop, making fake magazines or watching video tutorials for styling curly hair. I then decided to make my own video using my first gen phone camera and really old editing software. The next day at school I remember people playing it out loud to tease me, but I was proud of myself and I owned it.

One of the biggest things I've learnt from life is that if what you do doesn't give you joy or fuel your spirit, it won't last. You have to figure out your purpose, and everything you do should align to that. When I first joined social media I didn't see it as a job so it was exciting and fun—it was simply an outlet to express my love for natural hair.

A lot of people ask how I live the life I do with freedom, and I believe that making wise choices about where I want to be has inspired me to move with intention. I've always wanted to work in a creative space, but I knew I had to learn how to make it work from a business perspective and so signed up for classes and workshops to help with that.

Align yourself with people who inspire you, spend time in spaces that uplift you, and don't be afraid to do things alone. When friends couldn't come with me to events, it never stopped me from walking into a space alone. You never know who you'll meet and how they might impact your life. When you're in those spaces, ask questions and gain as much knowledge as you can. Your determination and perseverance will always be felt and acknowledged in a room filled with your people.

dream without limits

One of the most freeing things about being a child was the ability to dream with no limits. As we get older, the pressures of being financially stable or successful can sometimes cloud our dreams because we choose the safe option. But safety doesn't bring joy every day, nor does it fulfill all aspects of you.

I want you to immerse yourself back into the thoughts of your younger self when you weren't afraid of hearing the words "no" or "failure," when you didn't think about how you'd get somewhere, but you just knew you would. Let your mind guide you to that space and then think about what brings you joy.

We're all afraid of stepping out of our comfort zone because all we know exists only in our imagination; nothing is guaranteed. But that's the most exciting part about life! Where you'll be led will always empower you and teach you something that you wouldn't have learnt if you'd remained in your routine.

You have a purpose and you have a gift. Nurture them and watch yourself be nurtured. It's better to live a life knowing you tried something than to live with the feeling of wondering what might have happened if you'd believed in yourself.

write down your goals

Did you know that you're exactly where you're meant to be in this moment? You've grown through so much and you're still growing. Everything that's meant for you will come to you. You just need to trust in the process.

I've come to understand that things that aren't meant for me will never flow with ease, and that I need to let them go. Although we sometimes can't see the bigger picture, we're always aligned with where we're meant to go. But in order for us to know where we want to go, we must first acknowledge where we've been.

The first step in doing this is to write down your goals. Let them motivate and inspire you. You're destined for the greatness you keep dreaming about. All the things you're growing through now will help to make your future self stronger and wiser, so embrace pain, embrace discomfort, and embrace being sad. It's okay to feel all these emotions. We're all human.

Learn to be present in everything you do. When you're happy, embrace it. When you're sad, learn from it. When you're inspired, create with it. When you're tired, rest through it. Understanding that life is never going to be about consistent emotions is the moment you allow yourself to feel and grow.

Embrace where you are now. And remember, Queen, it's okay to have days of stillness, but on those days you should feel everything so that you don't take yesterday's problems into tomorrow.

I'll achieve

....
....
....
....
....
....
....

I'm proud of

....
....
....
....

I'll overcome my fear of

....
....
....
....

I'm capable of

....
....
....
....
....
....

nurture your dreams

The best thing you can do with any dream is start working toward it now. Thinking about it with positivity and affirmation is core to beginning your journey, and although you may not yet be where you want to be, you're on the right path now. You should feel proud of all the challenges you've overcome to reach this place.

Every time I think of a goal, it can be overwhelming to process how I'll reach it. But I also know that, for me, the most rewarding part of getting there is being able to look at back at all I achieved from just a thought or an idea.

Manifestation has been a really important part of my journey. It sets the tone and is a powerful tool to drive yourself and create a core sense of self-belief. I've achieved a lot, but nothing was handed to me and I had to use every part of my confidence to pitch myself to the right people or sign up for classes where I didn't know anyone. So many resources are available to help you embark on your new adventure, so take up a new hobby or nurture your dream. Sign up to everything and always trust that you'll be guided to the right place with the right people at the right time.

Hearing the word "no" can be scary, and that fear can hold you back, but we just need to understand the power of no. Sometimes it's the universe's way of steering us away from a path toward something better. Not everything will work out how you want it to, but it will always work out for the best.

manifest your dreams

Manifesting is a beautiful energy that you can create, but it's also important to act on what you want to achieve. For any goal I want to reach, I visualize the actions I'll need to take to lead me to that destination. So although it's great to imagine yourself living a life filled with adventure and freedom, also make a plan of how you can achieve that life. Write down your goal and a few steps that will help you get there. It all starts now!

My goal is:

_____

Steps that I can take are:

☐ _____

☐ _____

New habits I can include in my lifestyle are:

☐ _____

☐ _____

I can save money for my dream by:

☐ _____

☐ _____

stay true to your dreams

I've achieved many goals in exactly the way I manifested, but there are also goals that I didn't reach or that didn't align with who I am. I appreciate those too, because they taught me so much about what I should and shouldn't do. They strengthened my character and helped me make wise decisions in my career.

I was 16 when I started creating online content. It was just a hobby at the time, but I did it with love and passion. I didn't know that, years later, I'd be creating that same content with brands I loved and brands that would have felt unattainable to my younger self. No one took me seriously when I started out because I was so young and "still had a lot to learn" as people liked to emphasize.

There's no age that you should start chasing your dreams, nor is there an age at which you should stop. Do what feels right, but more importantly, do what makes you happy. If I'd listened to all those people who undermined me and told me I wasn't ready, who would have told me when I was ready? Only I knew that.

My mum advised me and often said, "There's no book to tell you how you should act at what age, and who you should be." I hope this book remedies that. Behind every page is an incredible team of women who believed in me. Had I not believed in myself, this book would still be an idea in my notepad. I was so excited when I first presented the idea out loud to the universe, but in bringing the book to the world I had to grow through letting go of people who didn't share the same core values as me, and every time I let someone go I felt like I was taking a step backward.

I wish I could see life from a full perspective to understand why things are happening at the time they are, but I'm learning to be patient and appreciate the mystery of the journey. I understand now why some people weren't meant to journey with me and my idea, but it took meeting the right people for me to see that.

With every goal you work toward, things may not flow as precisely as you envisage. It took me two years to sit down with a publishing company to pitch myself and my idea, and every time I did so I presented myself the best way I knew how, regardless of all the people who had declined my proposal in the past.

My career gives me the freedom to make many choices. Sometimes I'm offered work with a brand that's exciting or pays a lot of money, but it just doesn't reflect my values. When life throws an opportunity our way, sometimes it may not be for us. I'm a strong believer in doing things that align with your core beliefs because, in the long run, that's what you'll be remembered for.

Follow your light.
Follow your passion.
Follow your dreams.

what do you want to achieve?

At the start of every year I write a list of what I want to achieve in the 12 months ahead. Sometimes the list scares me, as I wonder how I'll achieve everything. But writing a list and seeing it in front of you can also inspire you and give you the push you need to bring your ideas to light.

I want you to write down all of your goals for the next year. Be as adventurous as possible and don't limit your thinking. It's better to dream big than live in a comfort zone. Nothing grows there.

Each month, check in with your list to see how you can move with intention to achieve everything on it. Although I'm a big believer in manifestation, it's also key to move with purpose. If you want to travel the world, have you started saving or reaching out to organizations about volunteering opportunities? If you want to achieve a certain grade at school, have you been revising or meeting with your tutors about specific subjects you need help with?

All of these things contribute to the bigger picture, but the first step is knowing the specifics of what you want to achieve.

In the next year I'll achieve...

☐ _____

☐ _____

☐ _____

In the next five months I want to...

☐ _____

☐ _____

☐ _____

By the end of this week I'll...

☐ _____

☐ _____

☐ _____

go with the flow

Achieving our dreams can be seen as glamorous as many people only see the end result—of a new product campaign, for instance—rather than seeing the scientists in the lab or the team trying to find new ideas for the visual concepts. So much time and effort are needed to achieve something, but that doesn't mean it's impossible.

Every time I feel worn out or overwhelmed by a goal I'm working toward, I take a step back to rest my mind. Resting is productive, too, and helps me to reset my creative and strategic abilities. You'll be presented with challenges, but when you experience them to their full capacity you'll know how hard you've worked and how much you can achieve when you push yourself and remain determined.

Don't allow the final goal you fantasize about to hinder your mind. Sometimes projects take unexpected directions, but flow with them and let them lead you to greater heights. For me, the hardest part about being a creative is accepting that there's no such thing as perfection. Learning this has allowed me to move with freedom when creating. When you have an expectation for a project you can limit yourself to greater possibilities.

Go with your own flow and embrace every part of the process. Your feelings and intuition will always guide you to the right path. As long as you trust yourself, you'll always be fine.

hold your vision

Whenever people ask me what drives me, I always say it's the ability to transform an idea into reality. There's so much power and strength in knowing that everything we use daily was once an idea. Some of the people who brought those ideas into being were called crazy for imagining an object that could fly to different parts of the world, or a device that could communicate with another through satellites. Those were both once just ideas, and if those ideas can become something big, then so can mine and so can yours.

My biggest dream is to open a school and home for young kids in Africa. My happy place is in Zimbabwe—it's the only place in the world where I cry with happiness every time I land, and experience that feeling of coming home. I wasn't born there, but it was born within me.

Although Zimbabwe gives me the feeling of home, for others that home is a place of poverty. Knowing that through my idea I can transform their home in years to come fuels me with so much energy, passion, and fear. Goals should never make you feel comfortable, they should challenge you to be better and do better for yourself and for the world.

I have a vision of me walking into the first assembly to tell the kids that they are here to learn, to have fun, and that this is a home that will elevate them to the next chapter in their lives. That vision keeps me going, because I know that one day it will happen.

One of my biggest achievements to date was in May 2018 when we built toilets for kids in Kenya. With the help of supporters we raised over £1,700 which transformed the facilities of a school. No brand campaign or ad I'd been part of had made me feel as empowered and fulfilled as I did then. Knowing that if I worked hard I'd achieve my vision was all the reward and motivation I needed to keep going.

My growth as a woman has come from challenges like these, and through each one I always learn so many amazing things about myself. Holding your vision is an important part of anything you want to achieve. It will always be there as a gentle reminder when things get tough and quitting seems like an easy option, or when you're still a few steps away from achieving your final goal.

You may not yet be where you want to be, but you're here now and that's enough. Keep evolving. Keep moving through life with the freedom to be who you want to be, doing what gives you that feeling of empowerment. This will come with challenges, but remember that each one will teach you something you need for the next part of your life. There's more value in the lesson than in dwelling on what might have been, so whenever something happens to you, focus on what it's trying to teach you.

chapter 6
self-love

Self-love is the most beautiful source of love that you can receive because it comes from you and no one can ever love you more than you can love yourself. After growing through many uncomfortable relationships and friendships, I've learnt that only I can love myself the way I want to be loved.

You set the standard for how you're treated and you create the boundaries for the love you will and won't tolerate. Setting high expectations for others to give you what you're not giving yourself is setting yourself up for disappointment. The only person you can ever have expectations of is yourself. You know your capabilities, and you know your strengths and weaknesses; the beauty in this is that you also know how you can improve, learn, and heal.

When was the last time you told yourself that you love yourself, or that you're more than capable of healing and evolving? When was the last time you encouraged yourself to go for that job and elevate your space to be around people who emulate positive energy, just like you? When was the last time you left a friendship or a relationship because it no longer served its purpose?

Affirmations have encouraged me during every step of my journey to womanhood. In this chapter, I've included a few challenges that encourage self-love. Have fun, and don't put too much pressure on yourself to get the challenges right straightaway; this is your book and your safe space, so you can come back to them when you're ready.

my journey of self-love

Self-love is the core of who you are. It's one of the most challenging experiences I've grown through as it involves far more than just looking after your exterior. It's learning to say, "no," learning to let go, and learning to know what you deserve.

My first understanding of self-love came when I was eleven years old and my godmother gifted me a book of affirmations. Before that, I thought it was rather vain for someone to love themself. But questioning that opinion led me to unlock this beautiful part of my life which has now inspired me to live with purpose and confidence.

Our self-love can be challenged daily by the way we choose to see ourselves when we first look in the mirror. My natural hair story sparked a beautiful journey of self-love, because until then I'd spent years learning to love parts of me, not the whole me. It was an unhealthy cycle and I became dependent on it to feel and look beautiful.

In order for us to grow and evolve, we have to experience discomfort. My dramatic moments of growth have come from not being happy with something, but now I'm in a space of always wanting to grow and work on aspects of myself, even when I'm perfectly comfortable with who I am. So, although I'm content with how I look, I still make the effort to work on my fitness, my diet, and even nurturing the people in my life.

I remember being on set for a global campaign shoot, one that would see my face in stores worldwide, and repeatedly apologizing for my acne and body hair. The photographer asked why I kept apologizing for things that were natural and I couldn't change right there on set. All I could change in that moment was how I felt about my skin, and once I realized that, I was able to walk on set with confidence and freedom. It was one of the most rewarding feelings.

I had to learn to stop apologizing because I was the only person who was ashamed of my body that day. If I hadn't mentioned my acne or body hair, no one would have said a thing.

Setting yourself a self-love routine is key. Establish an understanding of what you can do to improve the way you see yourself, and look inward to see what kind of person you are to yourself, what kind of friend you are to others, and what kind of daughter you are to your parents. It might be uncomfortable, but it will allow you to see how much room there is for growth.

For me to be the best version of myself for others, I must first be the best version of myself for me. Self-love is a journey and not a destination, so even when you work on something, another lesson will be waiting for you to learn and heal from.

the power of affirmations

When I began my self-love journey by using affirmations, they immediately sparked an interest in me to learn about and practice self-care. Words are powerful, from the ones you think in the far corners of your mind to the ones you speak into a space filled with people. Words enable you to touch someone without using your hands, and that power is sometimes undermined.

I was once booked for a self-love campaign that required me to write what I loved about myself on sticky notes before I went on set. At the time I was very low, and for a long time had depended on the words of others to boost my self-esteem. Writing these affirmations reminded me that I had power to describe how I saw myself, and this made me feel good.

Since then, I've practiced this form of self-care at my events and also in my journal whenever I've needed to give myself a boost of positivity. If we don't speak to ourselves with kindness, then how will anyone else do the same? I strive to live a life where I don't need the words of others to feed my soul.

As I journey through life, I know how I want to feel. I want to walk into a space feeling confident. I want to know my beauty and my strength. Affirmations have helped me to identify that only I can acknowledge who I am and who I want to be.

speak to your soul

I use affirmations to provide daily reminders that I can succeed and monthly encouragement that I'm evolving, both of which have been key to developing my confidence. Affirmations have contributed to my strength and helped me to realize that I'm capable of doing anything I put my mind to, and that when I'm down I'll always be okay.

The conversations you have with yourself are so important. Believing that you can achieve something or that you can heal through something is when your power truly begins to manifest. Whenever I'm down, I always speak to myself gently. I don't put pressure on myself to overcome something that I might need time to reflect on, or rush myself to get better if I'm sick.

Are you complimenting yourself and encouraging yourself to be better, or are you always diminishing your attributes, highlighting your flaws, and making yourself feel low? When other people compliment you, are you dimming yourself down or are you being open to receiving their love?

How would you describe yourself right now? Write only positive words down in the boxes opposite, or in your journal, and continue to describe yourself this way whenever you feel yourself going into a negative space. If you're a digital guru, then why not create a fun graphic for your phone wallpaper? Repeat your affirmations every morning and every night, and whenever you begin to doubt yourself. Repeat them when you're happy and when you're sad.

I am,...

....

I AM...

....

I AM...

....

I am,...

....

I AM...

....

I AM...

....

I am,...

....

I AM...

....

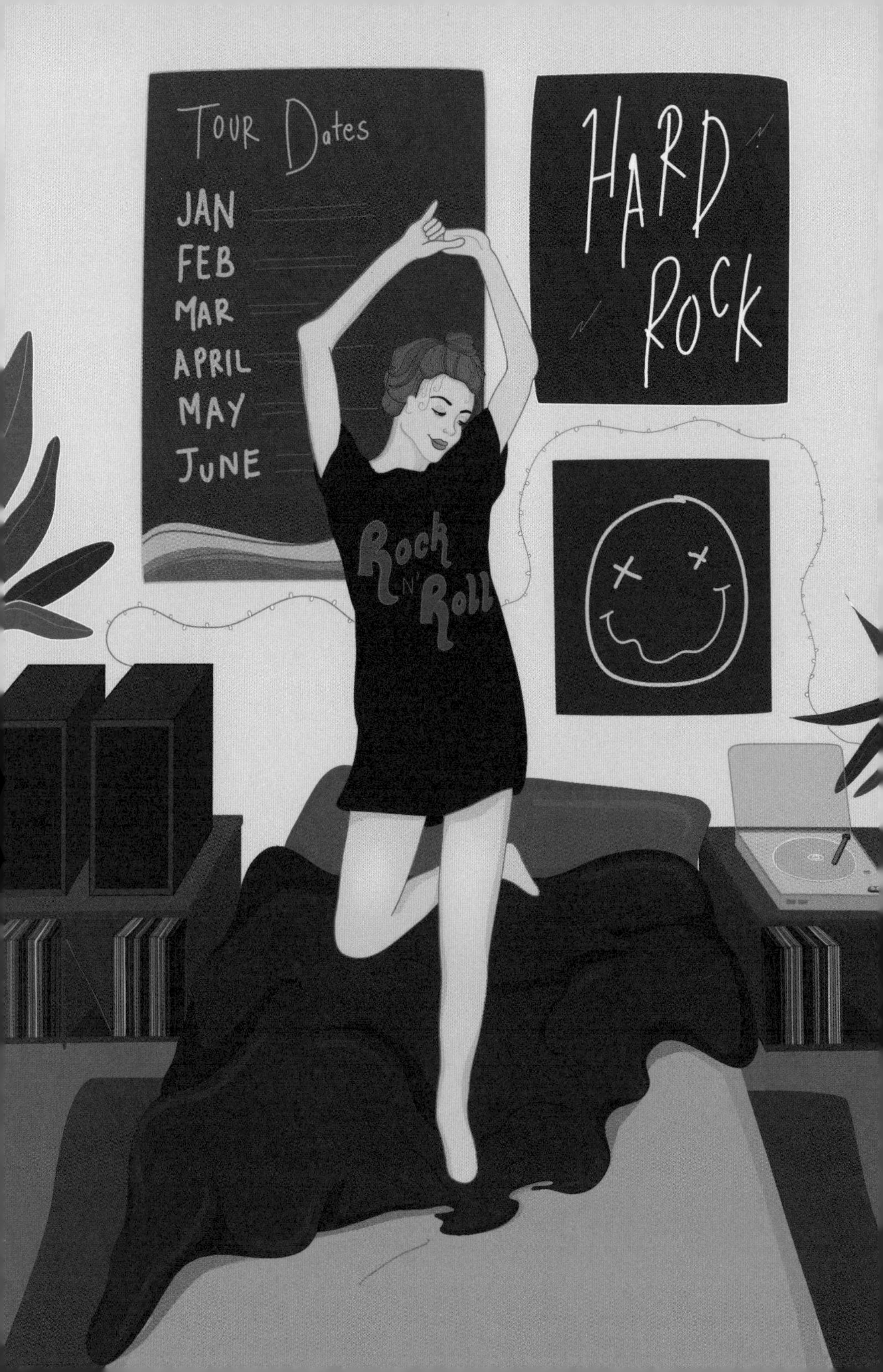

Tour Dates
JAN
FEB
MAR
APRIL
MAY
JUNE
HARD ROCK
Rock N' Roll

source of light

You're your own source of happiness. Create it and surround yourself with it. Don't depend on anyone else for happiness or a sense of validation as this can become unhealthy and toxic. Building a sense of self-love before receiving it from others is one of the most valuable lessons I've learnt. This journey takes time so don't feel any pressure to rush it.

I was once in a relationship on which I'd become dependent for confidence. At the time I thought confidence was what I needed, yet when my partner moved on I felt lost. I realized I needed to begin my journey from scratch, and I used this opportunity to reinvent my style and express my love for my natural hair with confidence and power. It was like having a new canvas to paint without worrying about anyone else's expectation of me.

As women, we were once taught that our value comes from our partner and their ability to see our worth. We were taught to wait to be complimented before complimenting ourselves, so as not to be vain or arrogant. It's time to unlearn this unhealthy behavior and focus on building and creating our own worth. Once I figured this out, I realized the importance of loving myself because no one can take this away. No one can take away your light.

It's a beautiful moment when you realize your worth, your power, and your purpose. The journey to reach that moment is even more rewarding, and it never ends. So enjoy your journey, and never take it for granted.

who do you aspire to be?

We all have a picture in our head of the future—how we want to look and where we want to live—but who do you want to be now? What aspects of yourself do you need to work on to get there? You could also create a collage with pictures and affirmations to help you.

What kind of friend do you want to be?

....

....

....

....

What kind of daughter do you want to be?

....

....

....

....

....

What kind of employee or student do you want to be?

....

....

....

....

What do you want to work on internally?

....
....
....
....
....
....
....
....

Which health choices do you want to improve on?

....
....
....
....

What does the older version of yourself look like to you?

....
....
....
....
....
....

No one can dim
your light unless
you give them the
power to do so.

embrace your identity

When I look back at my journey so far, it's so inspiring to see how much I've evolved over time. I love to see how many different hairstyles I've tried or how many outfits I've experimented with. Every day, I play dress-up and ask myself who I want to be. There isn't just one part to me; there never has been. I might be classy, cool, minimal, or abstract, but each look reflects who I am.

I've learnt the most about myself when I've been at my lowest. When I was down, my only option was to rise. In Chapter 1, I asked you to create a timeline of your life journey so that you could see how events impacted you and the woman you've become today. Some of my life experiences made me sensitive, but also taught me to be observant about whom I could trust. Some events made me feel proud, and gave me the energy to do more and achieve more for myself. We can't see the next parts of our timeline, but we can see how the events leading up to this moment have shaped us into the women we are today.

My most significant step in embracing my identity happened when I was seventeen. I was fresh out of my first break-up and, surprisingly, I wasn't heartbroken—I just felt free. I'd invested so much time fitting the mold that my partner created for me, and after our break-up I couldn't be comfortable with the idea of being anyone other than myself.

I realized that I hadn't been myself in a long time. I started to use the voice my partner tried to take from me, and I screamed for joy through my fashion and my style. It was so liberating. I also began wearing brighter, African-print clothing. It brought me closer to my Zimbabwean culture, and walking around London in these prints made in villages by women who emulate strength and beauty felt so freeing. I felt like I was truly embracing both sides of my culture.

As I've grown older and acquired more titles—businesswoman, a salon owner, big sister, graduate, godmother, auntie—I've learnt to express myself differently in each role. I like to feel all those roles and be the best I can at each one. The more we grow, the more we change how we see ourselves and how we reflect that to the world.

When I cut my hair, I wanted a fresh start—to see myself for who I was and to dive into any hidden gems that my hair had been concealing. It was something I needed to grow through, to be able to express where I was mentally and spiritually. The way I saw myself changed, as did the way I felt about myself. I began to see that I was more than just my physical self, and that I had a gift I could use to help change the world.

Each time I've been down or in a depressed mindset, I've always found an opportunity to recreate myself through that pain or use the energy to embark on a new project.

choose you

Life begins when you decide to be true to yourself, but that moment isn't always celebrated by everyone around you. Many people have tried to diminish me, but their words didn't impact me because I always chose myself, but in the process of doing so I had to let those people go.

I wasn't put on this Earth to meet anyone's expectations of me beside the ones I set for myself. Your purpose is far beyond making someone else happy. Sometimes we strive to make others happy as a form of self-validation. We know that, in return, they might reward us with words or comfort us with love, but we shouldn't have to change ourselves to make others happy. Choose your own destiny and let your passion push you into spaces you can't even imagine.

Each time I've embarked on a new project or wanted to strive to achieve something big, people around me projected their insecurities onto me. But I'm not the limitations they've set for themselves, nor am I living in the comfort zone they've designed for themselves. I'm limitless and deserving of everything I desire.

Choose you, always. Choose the career that you can see yourself waking up to with joy, and if you fall in love with another path, choose that too. Choose the hair color that will make you feel your most vibrant. Choose the shoes that bring you to life with every step you take. Choose you, Queen.

Choose your own destiny and let your passion push you toward it.

begin your journey now

Self-love is a journey, not a destination. Remember that every time you find yourself beating yourself up for not meeting the expectation you'd set for yourself. It's great to aspire to something and work hard, but you might not get it right first time and that's okay. Trying is the hardest part of the journey, but it's important to acknowledge that you did it and next time you'll know what you can do better. We all want to be perfect at everything we do because we feel like the end project or the end goal is the reward, yet that's never the end nor is it the reward as there will always be something to improve on.

I used to think that when I completed something I'd feel content, yet often this simply fueled me to do it again but better or to try something new. When I was sixteen, I started traveling by myself, touring around the world to bring women together. It all started in a park in London with some product sachets I'd collected from previous events. I bought snacks and picnic blankets and convinced several photographers I knew to film my event for free. I had no sponsors and no fancy backdrops for us to create content; it was just us, and that was enough.

Year after year the tours grew bigger, the venues became better, and the people who showed up came in abundance, but the love and the sense of community always stayed the same. If I hadn't had the self-confidence and passion to host it in a park, then I wouldn't have reached the fancy Cape Town house that enabled me to host one hundred women, or the beautiful Los Angeles studio that had live performances and a wall filled with affirmations.

But I had to start somewhere. Start now so that you'll never regret wishing you started yesterday. As long as you believe in yourself, you'll reach places that you didn't plan for or even dream of. Those who believe in you will join you on your journey and flow just as you do.

If I'd started my journey with the expectation of myself to get the sponsors or the fancy venues straightaway then I would've been disappointed in myself. But I never thought about those things because I organized every event out of love, and I held an image in my mind of a space filled with women who empowered and embraced each other.

Don't be hard on yourself when you need to rest or put down your laptop. Be patient with yourself and be kind to your mind.

Each time I've achieved something, I look back at the moments of stress or frustration when I reminded myself that everything would work out just as the universe intended it to. When things went wrong, I always found a way to make it right.

You will too, Queen. Just enjoy the ride!

love and light

That brings us here, Queen. It's the end of the book, but this isn't the end of your journey. I've enjoyed sharing my story with you and I hope you enjoyed reflecting on the sentimental parts of yours on each page. Remember that self-love is not a destination but a journey. There will always be room for growth within, so embrace it and acknowledge it. You may not be where you aspire to be, but you're here now and that's enough.

For all the Queens who are still learning to love their body: remember to thank it for enabling you to see and feel the world for what it is. Love it, cherish it, and feed it with nothing but the best. Your body is yours and you decide who deserves to share it with you.

To my sisters who are still creating and discovering who they are: have fun! Explore all the hair colors you want to try, dress in ways that reflect how you feel, and never be anything but yourself for you are the only person who knows what it means to be you.

For all the ladies who are still learning to love their scars and the lines that remind them of their growth: you are not defined by those things. They do not change the worth of you, nor do they validate you. They're simply a part of you. Own them and embrace them.

To the women who spend hours mastering their craft, balancing different jobs and tending to their education while raising siblings or children: I see you. We see you. You have our support, you have the strength to push through, and you will get there. Just be patient and always be proud of yourself. You're doing the best you can.

To my loves who are in love or still discovering love: I wish you nothing but beautiful memories with all the souls you welcome to your safe space. I wish your heart protection when it needs to let go, and I wish your mind freedom when it wants to see the world. Everyone in your life is placed to teach you something, and the lesson is the blessing. Learn it and let go.

Whenever you feel yourself deep in thought, I hope these pages provide a safe space to write and to feel. Give yourself time to be still for resting can be productive—it allows you to listen to your body and focus on self-care. Whatever that means for you, never forget to indulge in it. Make memories, have fun with your friends, see the world, and never forget to do what gives you joy.

Thank you to all the souls who were a part of this journey, from the lessons we learnt to the abundance of blessings we received. I manifest that one day we meet again through the beauty of words. I'm truly grateful to you for making it possible for me to fulfill this dream. I'm so proud of myself and I know that we will always be together through *The Book of Light*.

about nia

Nia the Light is a model, business owner, social media influencer, and above all a confidence and body-positive advocate for Queens everywhere learning to find their own bright journey through life.

Zimbabwean and British-born Nia Pettitt is a breath of fresh air in the YouTuber and global social media community. She's the creator of @niathelight, the Nia the Light YouTube channel, and @happyfroday (a celebration of natural hair), and CEO of The Curl Bar London.

> *"It started with a simple acceptance to love my natural hair which has somehow allowed me to grow as a person. Acceptance of your flaws and your imperfections leads to great things. Embrace who you are, embrace everything about you, embrace your flaws. They're what make you, you!"*

A Gemini, daughter, sister, and avid traveler, Nia takes her journey of self-love across the globe from the USA, Africa, and Dubai to Europe and her home town of London.

 **@niathelight**

 **@niathelight**

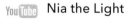 **Nia the Light**

 **niathelight.com**

HAY HOUSE
Look within

Join the conversation about latest products, events, exclusive offers and more.

 Hay House

@HayHouseUK

 @hayhouseuk

 healyourlife.com

We'd love to hear from you!